At the
Beach

by **Dana Meachen Rau**

Reading Consultant: Nanci R. Vargus, Ed.D.

 Marshall Cavendish
Benchmark
New York

Picture Words

beach

feet

goggles

kite

pail

sand

shells

sky

starfish

umbrella

waves

Let's go to the  .

See the  on

my 👣.

See my friend in the .

See my  in the

.

See the on my face.

See the  on
the rocks.

See the  in my .

See the  where we rest.

The  is fun.

20

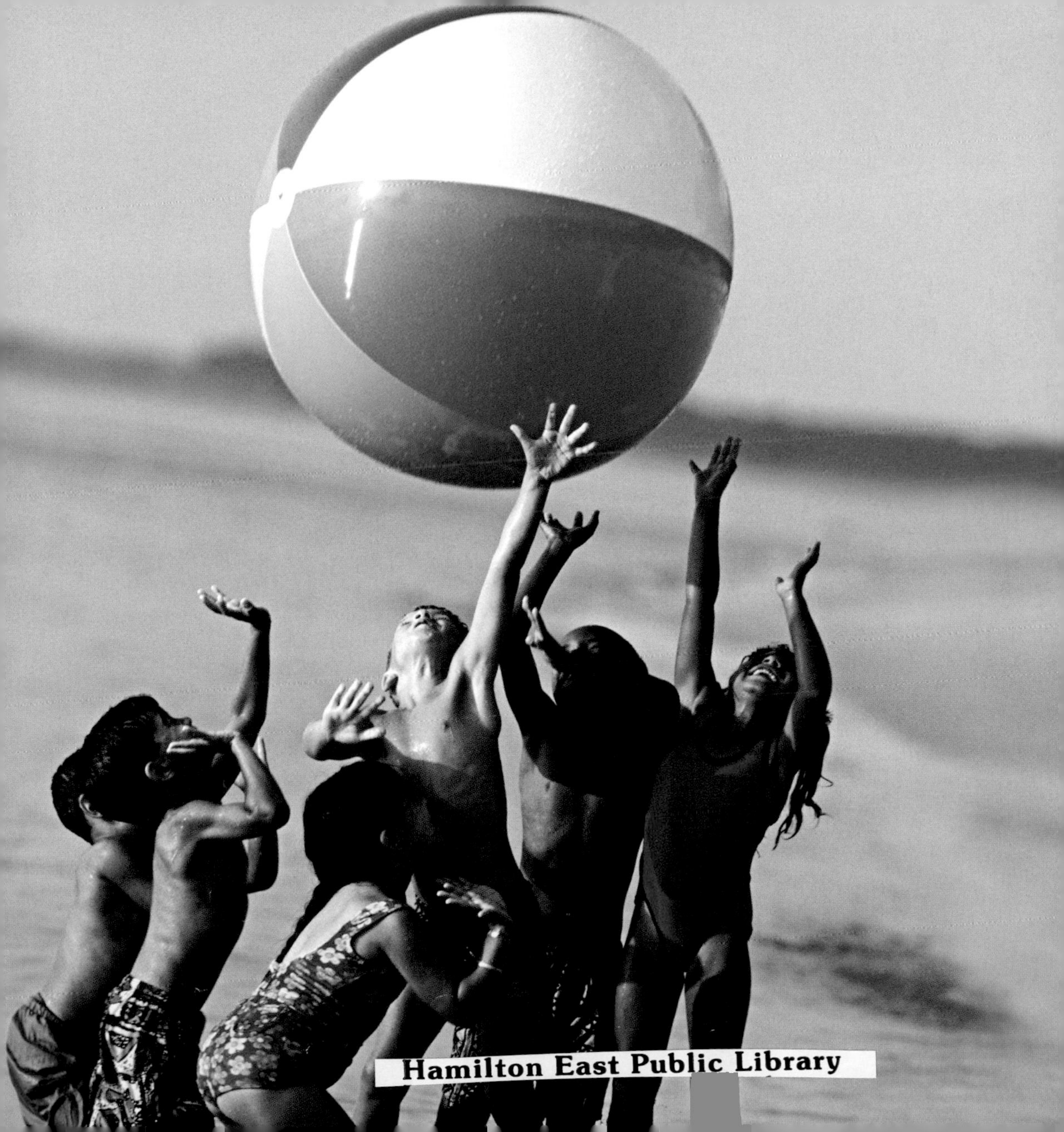

Words to Know

friend (frend)
a person who you like to spend time with

rest to take a break from an activity

Find Out More

Books

Berkes, Marianne. *Seashells by the Seashore*. Nevada City, CA: Dawn Publications, 2002.

Brenner, Barbara. *One Small Place by the Sea*. New York: HarperCollins Publishers, 2004.

Otten, Jack. *Watch Me Build a Sandcastle*. Danbury, CT: Children's Press, 2002.

Videos

Burton, LeVar. *Seashore Surprises*. GPN Educational Media, 2003.

Neale, Anne. *Amazing Seashore Animals*. DK Vision.

Web Sites

Kids Health for Kids: Swimming
http://www.kidshealth.org/kid/watch/out/water.html

Oceanlink: All About the Ocean
http://oceanlink.island.net/index.html

Sand Castle Central
http://www.sandcastlecentral.com/

About the Author

Dana Meachen Rau is an author, editor, and illustrator. A graduate of Trinity College in Hartford, Connecticut, she has written more than one hundred books for children, including nonfiction, biographies, early readers, and historical fiction. She likes to go to a lake near her home in Burlington, Connecticut, to play in the sand and water with her family.

About the Reading Consultant

Nanci R. Vargus, Ed.D., wants all children to enjoy reading. She used to teach first grade. Now she works at the University of Indianapolis. Nanci helps young people become teachers. Her favorite beach is on the Russian River in northern California.

Marshall Cavendish
99 White Plains Road
Tarrytown, NY 10591-9001
www.marshallcavendish.us

Copyright © 2008 by Marshall Cavendish Corporation
First Marshall Cavendish paperback edition, 2008

Library of Congress Cataloging-in-Publication Data

Rau, Dana Meachen, 1971–
At the beach / Dana Meachen Rau.
     p. cm. — (Benchmark rebus)
Includes bibliographical references.
ISBN 978-0-7614-3227-2 (PB)
ISBN 978-0-7614-2609-7 (HB)
1. Beaches—Juvenile literature. 2. Seashore ecology—Juvenile literature. 3. Vocabulary—Juvenile literature.
I. Title. II. Series.
GB454.B3R38 2007
551.45'7—dc22   2006028009

Editor: Christine Florie
Publisher: Michelle Bisson
Art Director: Anahid Hamparian
Series Designer: Virginia Pope

Photo research by Connie Gardner

Rebus images, with the exception of waves, provided courtesy of *Dorling Kindersley*.

Cover photo by Elyse Lewin/Image Bank/Getty

The photographs in this book are used with permission and through the courtesy of:
David Pu'u/CORBIS: p. 3 (waves); *Getty*: p. 5 Ian Royd; *PhotoEdit*: p. 7 Michael Newman; p. 9 Kayte M. Deloma;
p. 17 Mary Kate Denny; *Jupiter Images*: p. 11, *Corbis*: p. 13 Elenora Ghioldi; p. 15 Galen Rowell; p. 19 Reed Kaestner;
p. 21 Ariel Skelley.

Printed in Malaysia
1 3 5 6 4 2